LEVEL
2

# George Washington

Caroline Crosson Gilpin

NATIONAL
GEOGRAPHIC

Washington, D.C.

## For Joe Gardner —C.C.G.

The publisher and author gratefully acknowledge the helpful review of this book
by Jamie Bosket, vice president for interpretation at
George Washington's Mount Vernon.

Trade paperback ISBN: 978-1-4263-1468-1
Reinforced library binding ISBN: 978-1-4263-1469-8

Book design by YAY! Design

The picture on page 8 is from a museum exhibit at Mount Vernon: a lifelike model of
George Washington at age 19. The photo is from 2006.

Cover, (portrait) Museum of the City of New York/Corbis; (Background), Corbis; 1, Virginia Historical Society, Richmond, Virginia; 2, Henry Groskinsky/Time Life Pictures/Getty Images; 5, Universal History Archive/Getty Images; 6, jackhollingsworth.com/Shutterstock; 7, Jonathan Hodson/SuperStock; 7 (INSET), Mount Vernon Ladies' Association; 8, Mount Vernon Ladies' Association; 9, original painting by Charles Willson Peale/The Granger Collection, NY; 11 (UP), Bettmann/Corbis; 11 (LO), jackhollingsworth.com/Shutterstock; 12 (UP), sauletas/Shutterstock; 12 (LOLE), Jiang Hongyan/Shutterstock; 12 (LORT), Jiri Hera/Shutterstock; 13 (UP), Galushko Sergey/Shutterstock; 13 (LO), The Granger Collection, NY; 15, SuperStock; 16, Jonathan Hodson/SuperStock; 17, North Wind Picture Archives; 18, Fotosearch/Getty Images; 19 (LE), PoodlesRock/Corbis; 19 (RT), jackhollingsworth.com/Shutterstock; 20-21, original painting by Emanuel Gottlieb Leutze/Bettmann/Corbis; 22-23 (Background), Steve Collender/Shutterstock; 22 (UP), Glen Stubbe/ZUMA Press/Corbis; 22 (LO), tukkata/Shutterstock; 23 (UP), Mount Vernon Ladies' Association; 23 (CTR), Teubner Foodfoto/the food passionates/Corbis; 23 (LO), Stock Montage/Getty Images; 25 (INSET), SuperStock RM/Getty Images; 25, Bettmann/Corbis; 26, The Granger Collection, NY; 27, Universal History Archive/Getty Images; 28 (UP), Gurgen Bakhshetsyan/Shutterstock; 28 (CTR), Neftali/Shutterstock; 28 (LO), Visions of America/UIG/Getty Images; 29, Gary Blakeley/Shutterstock; 30 (LE), Robert Alexander/Archive Photos/Getty Images; 30 (RT), schankz/Shutterstock; 31 (UPLE), Jonathan Hodson/SuperStock; 31 (UPRT), Christie's Images/Corbis; 31 (LOLE), Historical Picture Archive/Corbis; 31 (LORT), Gurgen Bakhshetsyan/Shutterstock; 32 (UPRT), Fotosearch/Getty Images; 32 (CTR LE), Corbis; 32 (CTR RT), Superstock/Getty Images; 32 (LOLE), Hulton Archive/Getty Images; 32 (LORT), Bettmann/Corbis

Printed in the United States of America
13/WOR/1

# Table of Contents

# Who Was George Washington?

George Washington was the first President of the United States. He was a farmer, a soldier, and a hero. He helped America become a free country.

Portrait of George Washington

**WORDS TO KNOW**

**PORTRAIT:** A picture or painting of a person

5

# Growing Up

George was born on February 22, 1732, on a farm in Virginia to a large family. He spent much of his time with his older brother Lawrence.

Lawrence lived on a plantation (plan–TAY–shun)

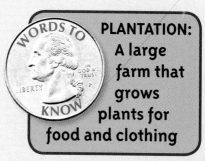

WORDS TO KNOW

PLANTATION: A large farm that grows plants for food and clothing

called Mount Vernon. He was an army officer. George wanted to be just like him!

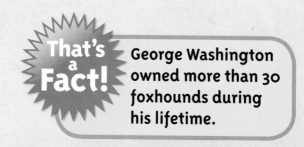

That's a Fact!

George Washington owned more than 30 foxhounds during his lifetime.

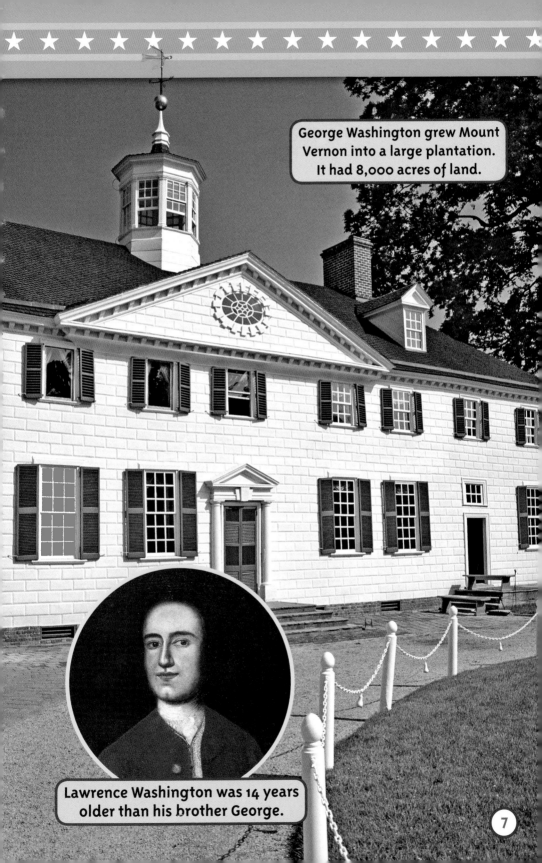

George Washington grew Mount Vernon into a large plantation. It had 8,000 acres of land.

Lawrence Washington was 14 years older than his brother George.

# Teaching Himself

When George was 11, his father died. He had to stop going to school to help at home. But George read a lot and taught himself. When he was 17, he got a job measuring land to make maps.

Measuring land was called "surveying" (SIR-vay-ing). It was an important job, and George did it well.

George was brave and strong. He was very good at riding horses. This helped him become a great soldier a few years later.

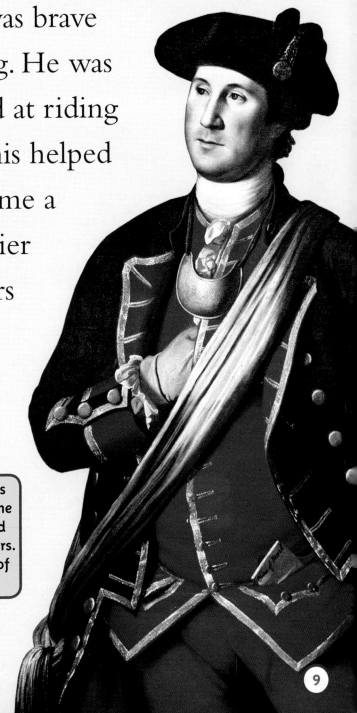

When George was just 23 years old, he was asked to lead the Virginia soldiers. This is a portrait of him in uniform.

# Becoming a Leader

In the 1700s, America was not yet the United States of America. It began as just 13 colonies (COL-uh-neez) ruled by King George III in England.

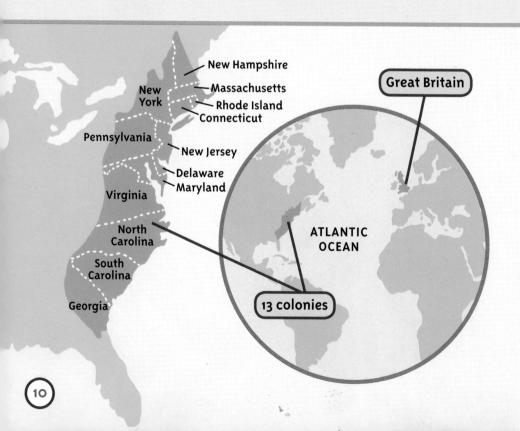

New Hampshire
New York
Massachusetts
Rhode Island
Connecticut
Pennsylvania
New Jersey
Delaware
Maryland
Virginia
North Carolina
South Carolina
Georgia
Great Britain
ATLANTIC OCEAN
13 colonies

King George III ruled England for 59 years! England is part of Great Britain. Wales and Scotland are also part of Great Britain.

People came on ships to live in America. They wanted more freedom than the king would give them in England.

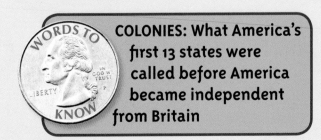

COLONIES: What America's first 13 states were called before America became independent from Britain

# In His Time

Many things were very different in the 1700s.

## Home

Many colonists (COL-uh-nists) lived on farms and built most of their own houses and furniture. They used homemade candles to light their rooms.

## Food

Most people grew their own vegetables, such as squash and peas. They hunted animals, such as deer and rabbits, for meat.

## Staying in Touch

There were no telephones. People used feather pens and ink to write long letters. The letters took weeks to reach the other person.

## Chores and School

Children helped with farm chores. Most children did not go to school. They learned to read and write at home.

# Mount Vernon

Sadly, when George was 20, his brother Lawrence died. Later, George became the owner of Mount Vernon.

In 1759, George married Martha Custis. They were happy together at Mount Vernon.

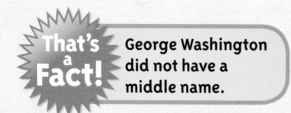

That's a Fact!
George Washington did not have a middle name.

Martha Custis and George Washington married ten months after they met.

# The Making of a Hero

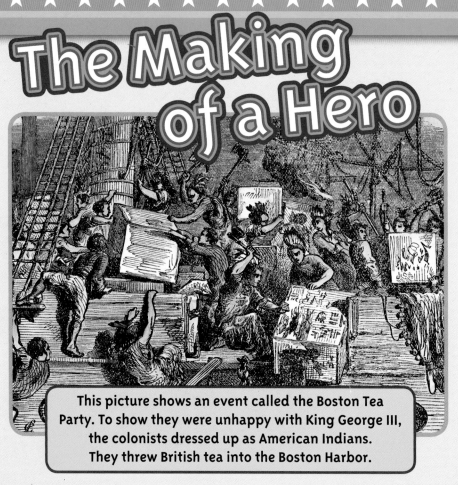

This picture shows an event called the Boston Tea Party. To show they were unhappy with King George III, the colonists dressed up as American Indians. They threw British tea into the Boston Harbor.

In the 1760s, there was trouble coming. King George III made the colonists pay extra money for tea and other supplies they needed. The colonists didn't think it was fair. They were angry.

They wanted freedom from England.
They asked George Washington to
lead the American army
against the British army.

George Washington was a great leader. He was smart
and brave. He strongly believed in American freedom.

# War and Peace

The Revolutionary (rev-a-LOO-shuh-nair-ee) War started in 1775. The British thought they would win. They had more men and supplies.

American soldiers didn't have enough food or warm clothes. But they would do almost anything for freedom.

The Declaration of Independence

In 1776, America's leaders signed the Declaration of Independence (dek-luh-RAY-shun of in-duh-PEN-dunce). It said America had a right to be free and to make its own rules. The British didn't agree. They sent more troops to fight.

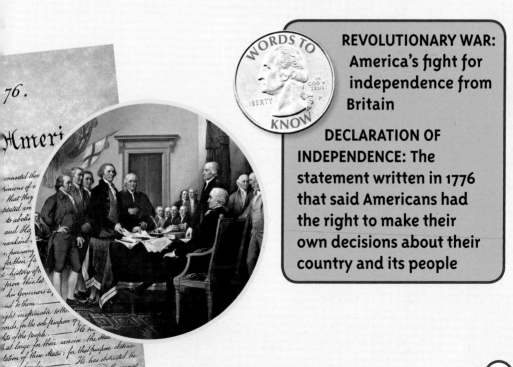

**REVOLUTIONARY WAR:** America's fight for independence from Britain

**DECLARATION OF INDEPENDENCE:** The statement written in 1776 that said Americans had the right to make their own decisions about their country and its people

For eight long years, the war
went on. The British were tired
of fighting a war far from home.

The British were beginning to run out of supplies and money. Finally, they gave up in 1783. America had won its freedom.

On Christmas Day in 1776, George Washington led his soldiers across the frozen Delaware River. They made a surprise attack on British troops the next morning. George's men won the battle. It gave them hope that they could win the war.

# 5 Cool Facts About George

## 1

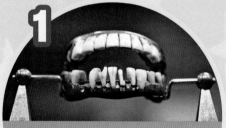

He had false teeth made from things like lead and ivory. He did not have wooden teeth!

## 2

He was born on February 22, but today most Americans celebrate his birthday on the third Monday of that month, often called President's Day.

**3**

He liked fox hunting on horseback. One of his favorite horses was named Blueskin.

**4**

He liked cornmeal pancakes (called "hoecakes") with butter and honey for breakfast.

**5**

He was very tall: almost 6'3". He had size 13 feet!

# Very First President

How would this new country work? In 1787, men from each state came together to write new rules for the United States. They called these rules the Constitution (CONS-ta-TOO-shun).

Then, they had to choose a new leader. George Washington was elected (e-LEKT-ed) the first President of the United States in 1789. It was a big job to unite the new country.

WORDS TO KNOW

UNITE: To bring together

## In Their Own Words

George Washington's friend Henry Lee III said that Washington was "first in war, first in peace, and first in the hearts of his countrymen."

George Washington became President on April 30, 1789. He didn't want to be called "King Washington" or have people bow to him. He chose to be called "President."

# Home Again

After eight years as President, George gave up his power. He was happy to go home to Mount Vernon again. He had many visitors. He rode his horses every day.

| **1732** | **1749** | **1755** | **1759** | **1775** |
|---|---|---|---|---|
| Born February 22 in Virginia | Takes a job measuring land | Becomes leader of the Virginia army | Marries Martha Custis | Revolutionary War begins |

In December 1799, George got sick with a bad sore throat. There was no medicine in his time to cure him. He was 67 years old when he died.

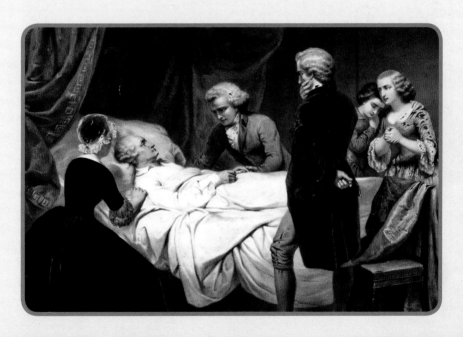

**1776**
Declaration of Independence written

**1783**
Revolutionary War ends

**1787**
U.S. Constitution written

**1789**
Elected first U.S. President

**1799**
Dies December 14

27

# In His Honor

George Washington was greatly loved. He is the only President to have a state named after him. His face is on the dollar bill, the quarter, and a U.S. postage stamp.

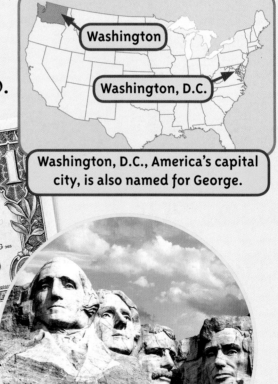

Washington, D.C., America's capital city, is also named for George.

George Washington is one of four Presidents carved in rock at Mount Rushmore National Memorial in South Dakota.

George Washington was the only President who did not live in the White House.

At 555 feet, the Washington Monument in Washington, D.C., is the world's tallest stone structure.

# What in the World?

Here are close-up pictures from George Washington's time. Use the hints below to figure out what's in each picture. The answers are on page 31.

**HINT:** The main way George Washington traveled from place to place

**HINT:** Paper money with Washington's picture

## WORD BANK

fox hunting    Martha Washington    horseback riding
Mount Vernon    dollar bill    Mount Rushmore

HINT: George Washington's home in Virginia

HINT: George Washington's wife

HINT: One of Washington's favorite outdoor activities

HINT: A famous place where George Washington is honored

Answers: 1. horseback riding, 2. dollar bill, 3. Mount Vernon, 4. Martha Washington, 5. fox hunting, 6. Mount Rushmore

**COLONIES:** What America's first 13 states were called before America became independent from Britain

**DECLARATION OF INDEPENDENCE:** The statement written in 1776 that said Americans had the right to make their own decisions about their country and its people

**PLANTATION:** A large farm that grows plants for food and clothing

**PORTRAIT:** A picture or painting of a person

**REVOLUTIONARY WAR:** America's fight for independence from Britain

**UNITE:** To bring together